PEGASUS ENCYCLOPEDIA LIBRARY

Space

SUN

Edited by: Pallabi B. Tomar, Hitesh Iplani
Managing editor: Tapasi De
Designed by: Vijesh Chahal, Anil Kumar, Rohit Kumar
Illustrated by: Suman S. Roy, Tanoy Choudhury
Colouring done by: Vinay Kumar, Kiran Kumari & Pradeep Kumar

CONTENTS

Introduction 3
Formation of the sun 5
Layers of the sun 7
The sun's magnetic field 9
Characteristics of the sun 10
Features 14
Solar eclipse 18
Sunlight 19
Sunrise and sunset 21
Sun's orbit 22
Solar space missions 23
Sun in culture 26
The fate of the sun 29
What the sun does for us 30
Test Your Memory 31
Index 32

Astonishing fact

All the coal, oil, gas and wood on Earth would only keep the sun burning only for a few days.

Introduction

Situated at the centre of the solar system, the sun is actually just a large star whose strong magnetic fields cause other solar matter, mainly planets, asteroids, comets, meteoroids and other debris, to orbit around it. The sun is believed to be more than 4.6 billion years old and is comprised of mostly hydrogen (74 per cent) and helium (25 per cent). The remaining 1 per cent is made up of small amounts of various heavier elements.

Life on Earth as we know it, would not be possible without the sun. The solar energy from the sun has supported and sustained terrestrial existence on Earth since the beginning of time. Plants utilize the sun to aid in photosynthesis. Humans and other mammals require energy from the sun for visual light, heat, as well as for powering modern solar devices. The sun is also directly responsible for determining and regulating the varying climates and weather cycles that occur on Earth.

The sun is the closest star to Earth and is the centre of our solar system. A giant, spinning ball of very hot gas, the sun is fuelled by nuclear fusion reactions. The sun is also an active star that displays sunspots, solar flares, erupting prominences, and coronal mass ejections. In about five billion years, the sun will evolve into a Red Giant and eventually, a White Dwarf star. Many cultures have had interesting myths about the sun, in recognition of its importance to life on Earth.

Only about 5 per cent of stars in the Milky Way are larger than the sun; the vast majority are smaller red dwarf stars. Some of the biggest stars can be 100,000 times brighter and contain 100 times more mass. The sun is also relatively young, a member of the Population I group of stars. Older stars, which formed billions of years before the sun are Population II stars and have less heavier elements in them. The oldest stars are Population III stars, formed just after the Big Bang, but these are purely theoretical.

Astonishing fact

The sun travels around the galaxy once every 200 million years – a journey of 100,000 light years.

Formation of the sun

Though exact information of the formation of the sun is not available, it is believed that it formed between ten and twenty thousand million years ago. As per the astronomers, the hydrogen gas present in the sun came into existence with the 'Big Bang'. In other words, the sun came into being around the same time as the rest of the universe. At the time of the Big Bang, hydrogen gas condensed to form colossal clouds, which later concentrated and formed the numerous galaxies. Some of the hydrogen gas was left free and started floating around in our galaxy.

With time, due to some incident, this free-floating hydrogen gas concentrated and paved way for the formation of the sun and the solar system. Gradually, the sun and the solar system turned into a slowly spinning molecular cloud, composed of hydrogen and helium molecules, along with dust. The cloud started to undergo the process of compression, as a result of its own gravity. Along with the compression, the rotating speed of the cloud became much faster. Its excessive and high-speed spinning ultimately resulted in its flattening into a giant disc.

Astonishing fact

The sun provides our planet with 126,000,000,000,000 horsepower of energy every day!

Majority of the mass of the disc started collecting right at its centre, resulting in the creation of a gas sphere. The sphere continued to attract material from the disc, which resulted in its further compression. This led to an increase in the temperatures and pressures inside the sphere, which rose to the extent where atoms started fusing in its very centre. This is the point of time when a star—the sun, formed, from the sphere. The rest of the disc, apart from the sphere, turned into planets and the other components of the solar system.

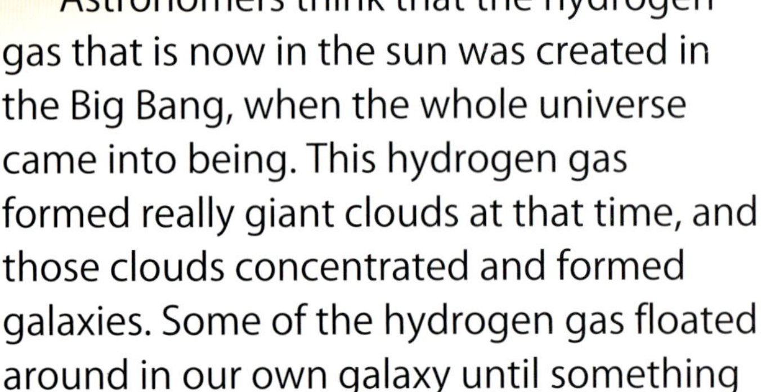

Astonishing fact

More than 1 million Earths would fit inside the sun!

Astronomers think that the hydrogen gas that is now in the sun was created in the Big Bang, when the whole universe came into being. This hydrogen gas formed really giant clouds at that time, and those clouds concentrated and formed galaxies. Some of the hydrogen gas floated around in our own galaxy until something made it concentrate and form the sun and the solar system.

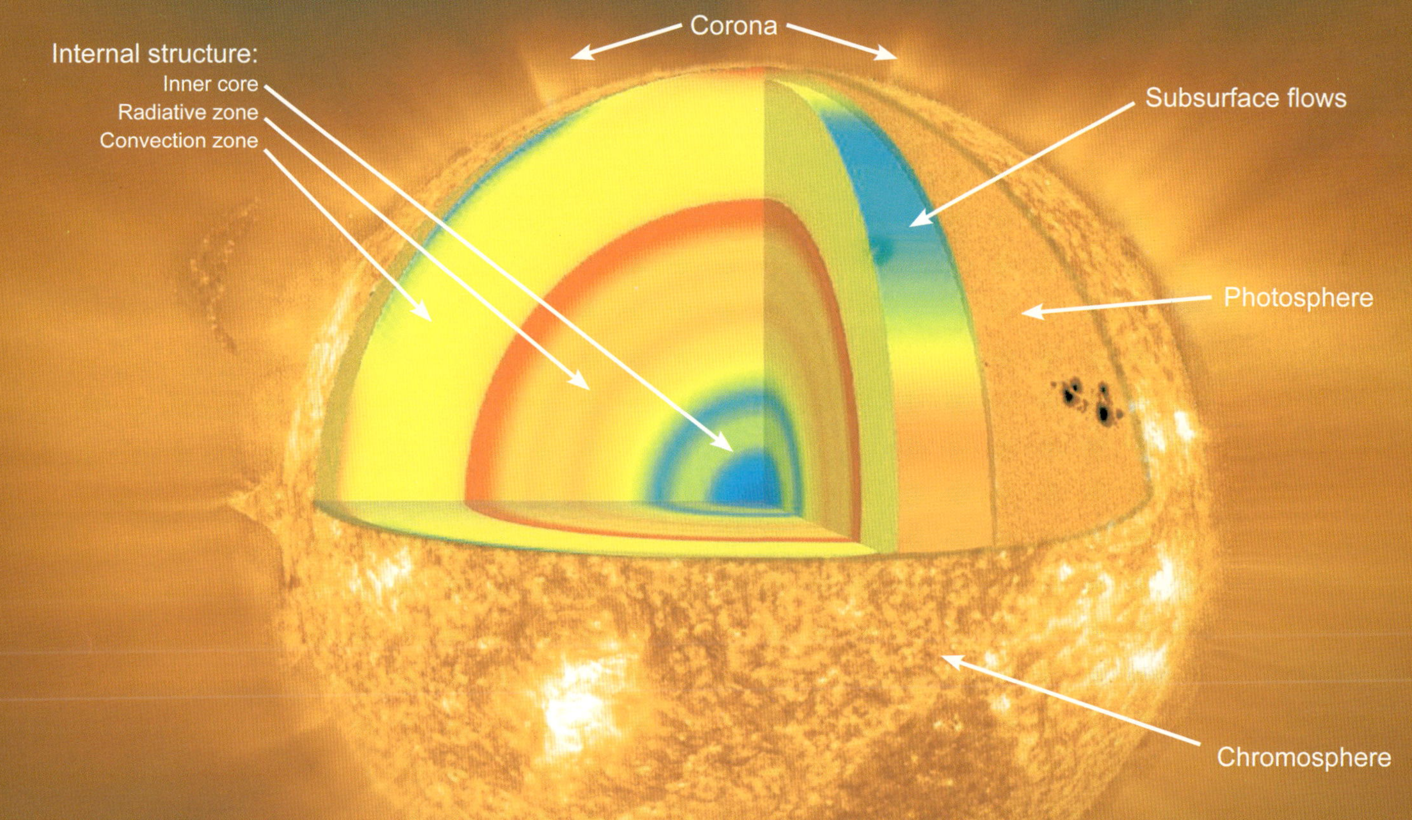

Layers of the sun

The sun is the closest star to Earth, at a mean distance from our planet of 149.60 million km. This distance is known as an Astronomical Unit (abbreviated AU), and sets the scale for measuring distances all across our solar system.

The sun is held together by gravitational attraction producing immense pressure and temperature at its core. The sun has six regions—the core, the radiative zone, and the convective zone in the interior; the visible surface, the photosphere; the chromosphere; and the outermost region, the corona.

At the **core**, the temperature is about 15 million degree Celsius, which is sufficient to sustain thermonuclear fusion. The energy produced in the core powers the sun and produces essentially all the heat and light we receive on Earth. Energy from the core is carried outward by radiation, which bounces around the **radiative zone**, taking about 170,000 years to get from the core to the convective zone. The temperature drops below 2 million degree Celsius in the **convective zone**, where large bubbles of hot plasma (a soup of ionized atoms) move upwards.

Astonishing fact

99 per cent of our solar systems mass is concentrated in the sun.

The sun's surface, the photosphere is a 500 km thick region, from which most of the sun's radiation escapes outward and is detected as the sunlight we observe here on Earth about eight minutes after it leaves the sun. Sunspots in the photosphere are areas with strong magnetic fields that are cooler and thus darker than the surrounding region. The number of sunspots goes up and down every 11 years as part of the sun's magnetic activity cycle. Also connected to this cycle are bright solar flares and huge coronal mass ejections that blast off the sun.

The temperature of the photosphere is about 5,500 degree Celsius. Above the photosphere lie the tenuous chromosphere and the corona ('crown'). Visible light from these top regions is usually too weak to be seen against the brighter photosphere, but during total solar eclipses, when the Moon covers the photosphere, the chromosphere can be seen as a red rim around the sun while the corona forms a beautiful white crown with plasma streaming outward, forming the points of the crown.

Astonishing fact

The sun is 330,330 times larger than the Earth!

Astonishing fact

For 186 days one cannot see the sun in the North Pole.

The sun's magnetic field

The sun is a magnetically active star. It supports a strong, changing magnetic field that varies year-to-year and reverses direction about every eleven years around solar maximum. The sun's magnetic field leads to many effects that are collectively called solar activity, including sunspots on the surface of the sun, solar flares, and variations in solar wind that carry material through the solar system. Effects of solar activity on Earth include auroras at moderate to high latitudes, and the disruption of radio communications and electric power. Solar activity is thought to have played a large role in the formation and evolution of the solar system.

All matter in the sun is in the form of gas and plasma because of its high temperatures. This makes it possible for the sun to rotate faster at its equator (about 25 days) than it does at higher latitudes (about 35 days near its poles). The differential rotation of the sun's latitudes causes its magnetic field lines to become twisted together over time, causing magnetic field loops to erupt from the sun's surface and trigger the formation of the sun's dramatic sunspots and solar prominences. This twisting action creates the solar dynamo and an 11-year solar cycle of magnetic activity as the sun's magnetic field reverses itself about every 11 years.

The solar magnetic field extends well beyond the sun itself. The magnetized solar wind plasma carries sun's magnetic field into the space forming what is called the **interplanetary magnetic field**.

Characteristics of the sun

Chemical composition

The sun, like most other stars, is made up mostly of atoms of the chemical element hydrogen. The second most plentiful element in the sun is helium and almost all the remaining matter consists of atoms of seven other elements. For every 1 million atoms of hydrogen in the entire sun, there are 98,000 atoms of helium, 850 of oxygen, 360 of carbon, 120 of neon, 110 of nitrogen, 40 of magnesium, 35 of iron, and 35 of silicon. So about 94 per cent of the atoms are hydrogen, and 0.1 per cent are elements other than hydrogen and helium.

But hydrogen is the lightest of all elements, and so it accounts for only about 72 per cent of the mass. Helium makes up around 26 per cent.

The inside of the sun and most of its atmosphere consist of plasma. Plasma is basically a gas whose temperature has been raised to such a high level that it becomes sensitive to magnetism. Scientists sometimes emphasize the difference in behaviour between plasma and other gases. They say that plasma is a fourth state of matter, alongside solid, liquid and gas.

Astonishing fact

Twice during Mercury's orbit, it gets so close to the sun and speeds so much that the sun seems to go backwards in the sky.

Size

The sun is 1,390,000 km in diameter that compares with 12,756 km for diameter of the Earth. In other words, the diameter of the sun is over 100 times the diameter of the Earth. This is equal to 109 Earth diameters and almost 10 times the size of the largest planet, Jupiter. All of the planets orbit the sun because of its enormous gravity. It has about 333,000 times the Earth's mass and is over 1,000 times as massive as Jupiter. It has so much mass that it is able to produce its own light. This feature is what distinguishes stars from planets.

Mass

The mass of the sun is about 2 x 1030 kg (2 followed by 30 zeros). It is one of the larger stars in our Milky Way galaxy. The mediam size of stars in our galaxy is less than half the mass of the sun. In comparison, the Earth is 6 x 1024 kg. This means that the mass of the sun is over 300,000 times greater than that of the Earth.

Distance

The sun is 149,600,000 km from the Earth. Since the speed of light is 303,000 km/sec, it takes the light slightly over 8 minutes to get from the sun to the Earth.

The distance of the sun to the Earth is called an Astronomical Unit (AU) and is sometimes used to denote large distances that are less than a light year.

Astonishing fact

If the sun were the size of a beach ball then Jupiter would be the size of a golf ball and the Earth would be as small as a pea!

Rotation

The sun rotates on its axis, which is approximately the same axis that most of the planets revolved around the sun. Since the sun is primarily made of very hot gas, the surface at the equator rotates once every 25.4 days. The rotation near the poles takes around 36 days. Also the surface swirls in high and low pressure areas, similar to those that occurs on Earth.

Temperature

Its temperature is extremely hot, with the surface being about 5000 degree Celsius and the centre core at 15,600,000 degree Celsius. The high temperature of the core, along with extreme pressure from the sun's mass, result in nuclear fusion reactions.

Radiation

The energy released from the fusion reactions near the sun's core is in the form of very high frequency electromagnetic waves called gamma rays.

As this radiation moves towards the sun's surface, it is absorbed by atoms in the sun's interior. After absorption, the rays are then re-emitted at lower frequencies. This process continues until the radiation reaches the sun's surface. By that time it is primarily visible light.

Astonishing fact

A comet's tail begins to melt as it nears the sun. A vast plume of gas millions of km across is blown out behind by the solar wind. The tail is what you see, shining as the sunlight catches it.

Energy output

Most of the energy emitted by the sun is visible light and a related form of radiation known as infrared rays, which we feel as heat. Visible light and infrared rays are two forms of electromagnetic radiation. The sun also emits particle radiation, made up mostly of protons and electrons.

Colour

In popular culture, the sun is yellow. But the colour of the sun is actually white. It's only when light from the sun passes through the Earth's atmosphere that it changes in colour, from white to yellow.

Astonishing fact

Hipparchus was the first astronomer to try to work out and see how far away the sun actually is.

The atmosphere of the Earth scatters sunlight, removing the shorter wavelength light – blue and violet. Once you reduce those colours from the spectrum of light coming from the sun, it appears more yellow. But if you could fly up and see the sun from space, the colour of the sun would be pure white.

Astonishing fact

The luminosity of the sun is equivalent to the luminosity of 4 trillion trillion light bulbs of 100 watt!

Features

Solar flares

A solar flare is a thunderous explosion that occurs in the solar corona and chromosphere within the atmosphere of the sun. The incredible energy level of a solar flare is equivalent to tens of millions of atomic bombs exploding at the same time!

Solar flares were first known to be occurring in 1859. Solar flare activity can vary from several per day to only a few a month, depending mostly upon the overall activity of the sun as a whole. Solar activity generally varies on an 11-year cycle. At the peak of this 'solar cycle' there are typically more sunspots on the surface of the sun, which ultimately leads to more frequently occurring solar flares.

Solar flares are typically classified as A, B, C, M or X, depending upon the degree of their peak flux. Most solar flares occur in or around sun spots as the result of intense magnetic fields emerging from the sun's surface into the corona. The powerful energy commonly associated with solar flares can take as long as several days to build up, but only minutes to release.

Solar wind

Solar wind is a continuous stream of matter that flows outward from the sun in all directions. The solar wind is composed of electrically charged particles primarily electrons and the nuclei of hydrogen and helium atoms. The particles travel away from the sun at speeds of 320 to 960 km/sec. Relatively few of the particles reach the Earth's atmosphere because the Earth's magnetic field acts as a barrier. Increases in the intensity of the solar wind are associated with auroras, magnetic storms, and other disturbances in the Earth's magnetic field and atmosphere.

It takes the solar wind about 4.5 days to reach Earth; it has a velocity of about 400 km/sec. Since the particles are emitted from the sun as the sun rotates, the solar wind blows in a pinwheel pattern through the solar system. The solar wind affects the entire solar system, including buffeting comets' tails away from the sun, causing auroras on Earth (and some other planets), the disruption of electronic communications on Earth, pushing spacecraft around, etc.

Astonishing fact

The amount of energy reaching the Earth's surface from the sun is 6,000 times the amount of energy used by all human beings worldwide.

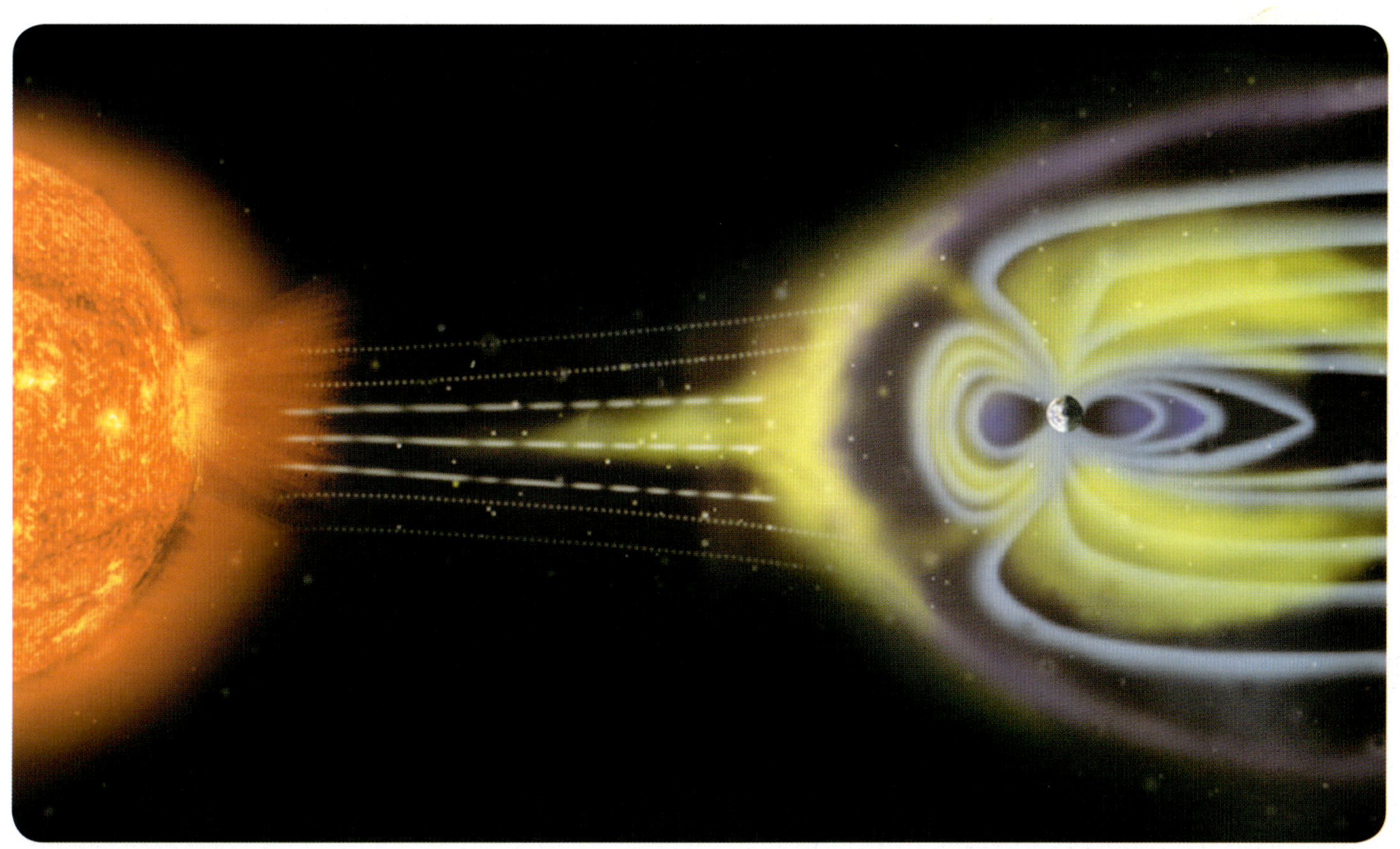

Solar prominence

A solar prominence is an arc of gas that erupts from the surface of the sun. It is often shaped as a loop and although actually very large, cannot be seen without the aid of a strong telescope and some filters. Prominences can loop hundreds and thousands of miles into space. Prominences are held above the sun's surface by strong magnetic fields and can last for many months. At some time in their existence, most prominences will erupt, spewing enormous amounts of solar material into space. The largest ever to be observed was estimated to be 350,000 km long. That's nearly ten times the entire circumference of the Earth!

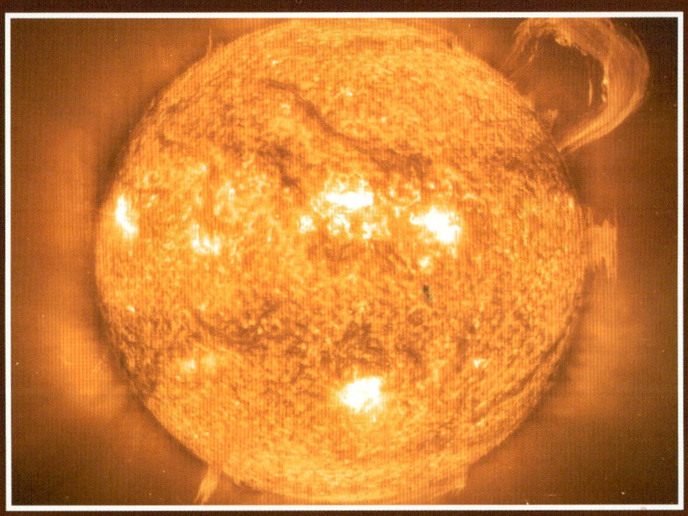

Astonishing fact

In Spitsbergen, Norway, at one time of the year the sun shines continuously for three and a half months.

Coronal mass ejections

Coronal mass ejections (abbreviated CME's) are huge, balloon-shaped plasma bursts that come from the sun. As these bursts of solar wind rise above the sun's corona, they move along the sun's magnetic field lines and increase in temperature up to tens of millions of degrees. These bursts release up to 100 billion kg of plasma. CME's can disrupt Earth's satellites. CME's usually happen independently, but are sometimes associated with solar flares.

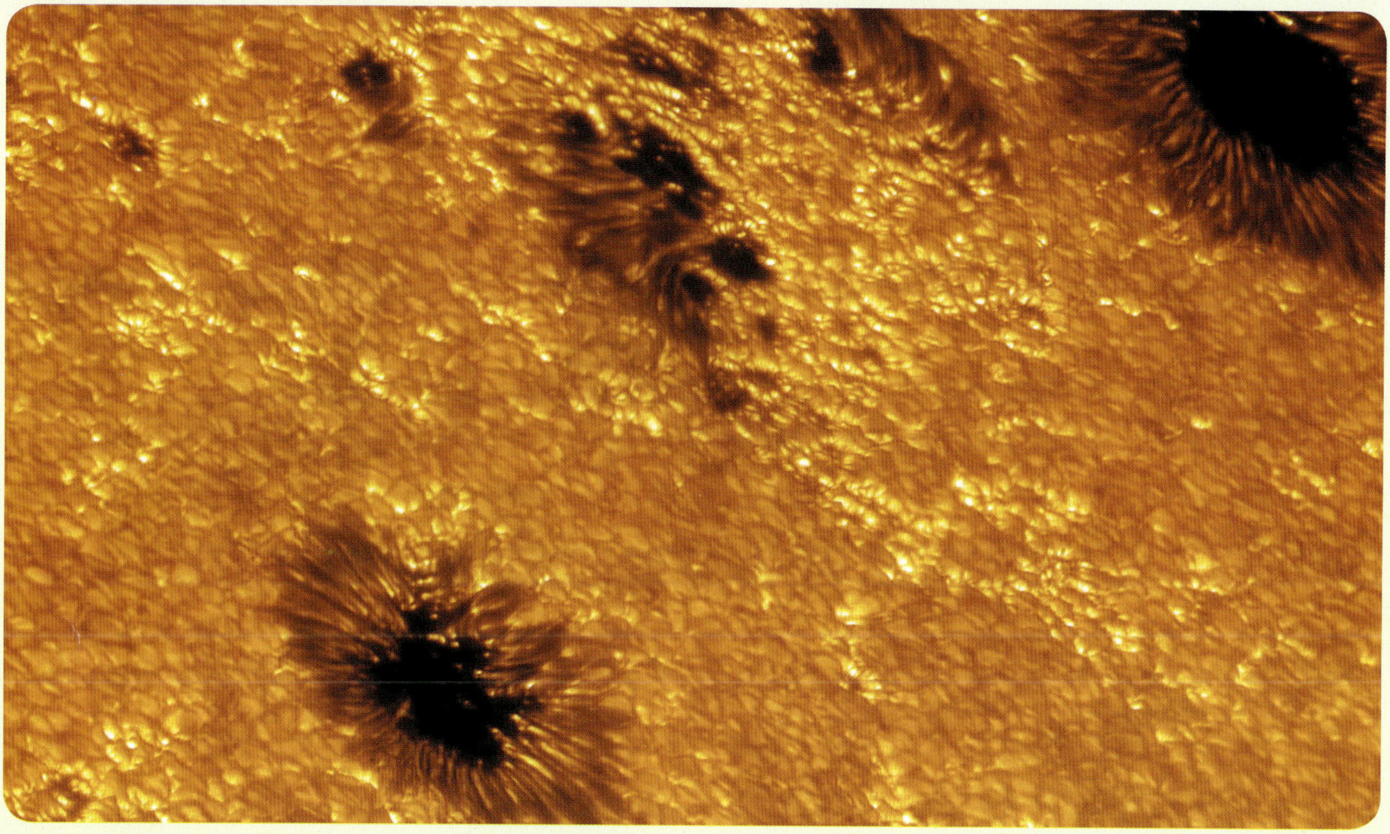

Sunspots

Sunspots appear as dark spots on the visible surface of the sun. Temperatures in the dark centres of sunspots drop to about 3700 K (compared to 5700 K for the surrounding photosphere). They typically last for several days, although very large ones may live for several weeks. Sunspots are magnetic regions on the sun with magnetic field strengths thousands of times stronger than the Earth's magnetic field. Sunspots usually come in groups with two sets of spots. One set has positive or north magnetic field while the other set has negative or south magnetic field. The field is strongest in the darker parts of the sunspots— the umbra. The field is weaker and more horizontal in the lighter part— the penumbra. The largest sunspot ever recorded was visible in March and April 1947 and covered an area of over 18,000 million square km; about a hundred Earths could be fitted into this area!

Sunspot activity occurs as part of an 11-year cycle called the solar cycle where there are periods of maximum and minimum activity.

Astonishing fact

An area on the sun's surface of the size of a postage stamp shines with a power of 1,500,000 candles!

Solar eclipse

A solar eclipse occurs when the moon, during its monthly trip around the Earth, happens to line up exactly between the Earth and the sun, so that it casts a shadow on the Earth. But because of the sun's large diameter, the shadow consists of two regions. The innermost cone of total darkness is called the umbra (Latin for 'shadow'), and it is projected in the centre. Anyone in this central area will observe the total eclipse, because the sun will be temporarily obscured by the moon. The outer shadow is partially illuminated by the sun and is called the penumbra. Anyone in this region will see the partial eclipse, since the sun is only partially obscured by the moon.

The glory of a solar eclipse comes from the dramatic view of the sun's corona or outer atmosphere, which we can see only when the brilliant solar disc is blocked by the moon. The corona is not just light shining from around the disk. It is actually the outermost layer of the solar atmosphere. Although, the gas is very sparse, it is extraordinarily hot (800,000 to 3,000,000 K), even hotter than the surface of the sun! The corona shows up as pearly white streamers and their shape is determined by the sun's current magnetic fields. Thus every eclipse will be unique and beautiful in its own way.

Astonishing fact

The energy being emitted from 1 square cm of the sun's surface is enough to burn 64 light bulbs of 100 watt.

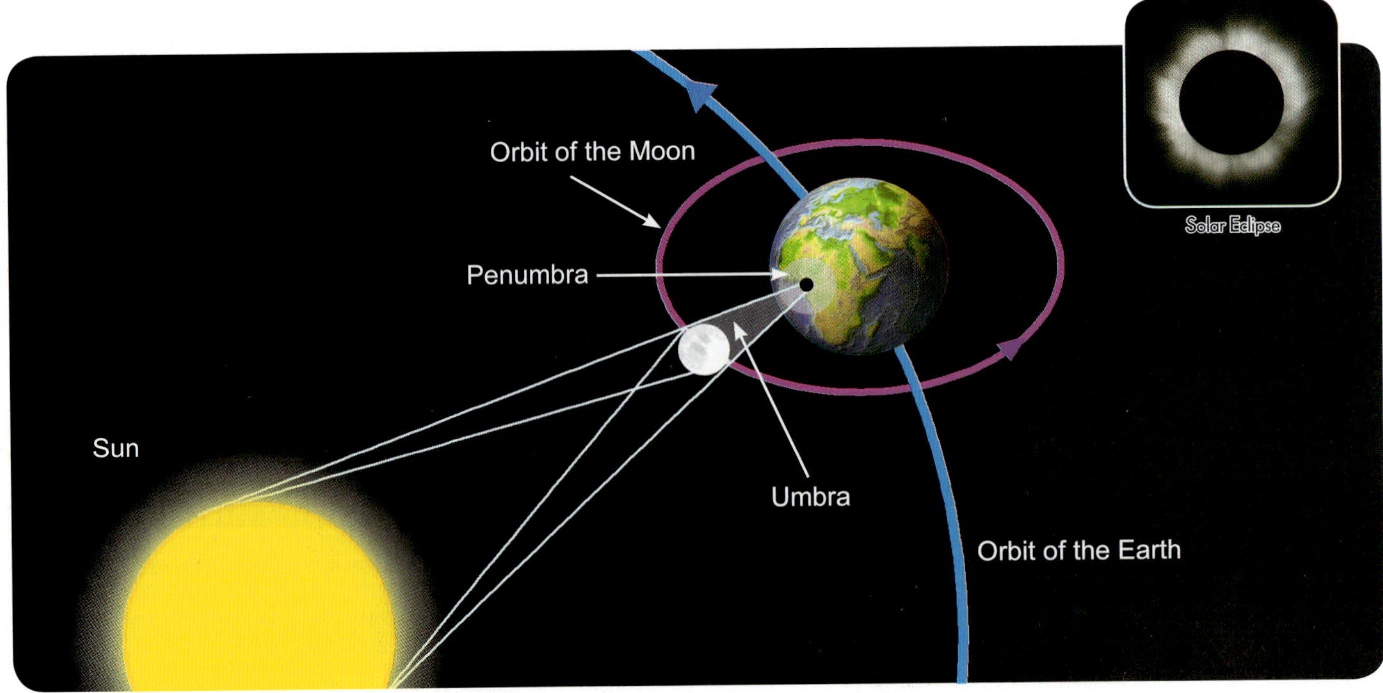

Astonishing fact

The light from the sun takes 5.5 hours to travel to Pluto.

Sunlight

Sunlight is the general term for all of the electromagnetic radiation emitted by the sun. Although we see the sun with our eyes in the visible spectrum, the sun is actually releasing everything from radio waves and infrared to ultraviolet and even X-ray radiation. Satellites in orbit estimate that the total amount of sunlight that reaches Earth is about 1.366 kilowatts per square metre.

The Earth is located at an average distance of about 150 million km from the sun. It takes sunlight about 8.3 minutes to cross this distance and reach the Earth. When the sunlight reaches Earth, it's partly absorbed by the Earth's atmosphere. Whatever reaches the ground helps to warm the Earth, and keep it hospitable for life.

The amount of sunlight that the Earth receives changes over the course of the year. This is because the Earth orbits the sun in an elliptical orbit. At its closest point, the Earth actually receives 1.413 kW/m^2, and then at the most distant point of its orbit, the Earth only receives 1.321 kW/m^2.

Planets further away from the sun receive less sunlight. Mars only gets about 550 kW/m^2, while Neptune only receives 1.5 kW/m^2.

Sunlight is Earth's primary source of energy. The solar constant is the amount of power that the sun deposits per unit area that is directly exposed to sunlight. The solar constant is equal to approximately 1,368 W/m^2 at a distance of one astronomical unit (AU) from the sun (that is, on or near Earth). Sunlight on the surface of Earth is attenuated by the Earth's atmosphere so that less power arrives at the surface—closer to 1,000 W/m^2 in clear conditions when the sun is near the zenith.

Solar energy can be harnessed by a variety of natural and synthetic processes—photosynthesis by plants captures the energy of sunlight and converts it to chemical form (oxygen and reduced carbon compounds), while direct heating or electrical conversion by solar cells are used by solar power equipment to generate electricity or to do other useful work. The energy stored in petroleum and other fossil fuels was originally converted from sunlight by photosynthesis in the distant past.

Astonishing fact

The total amount of fossil fuel used by humans since the first civilization is equivalent to less than 30 days of energy reaching the Earth's surface from sun.

Sunrise and sunset

Although, it looks like the sun is moving through the sky from our vantage point, it's actually the Earth's rotation on its axis that causes the apparent motion of the sun. And that's why we have sunrise and sunset.

Astronomers consider sunrise to be the moment when the leading edge of the sun first peeks up over the horizon in the east. Sunset happens when the sun's trailing edge completely disappears over the horizon in the west.

The sunrise and the sunset times are different for every place on the Earth. It depends on your day of the year, your distance from the equator, and your position within the time zone. That's why sunrise sunset times can be a few minutes different from other locations.

When the sun is just setting or rising, we see it passing through the largest amount of the Earth's atmosphere. As the light passes through this larger amount of atmosphere, the red and orange portions of the light scatter more easily when they encounter particles in the atmosphere. This is why sunrise and sunset can be spectacular, with the beautiful orange and red colours in the sky.

Astonishing fact

The sun is one among the 6000 stars which is visible to the naked eye from the Earth.

Sun's orbit

Astronomers have calculated that it takes the sun 226 million years to completely orbit around the centre of the Milky Way. In other words, that last time that the sun was in its current position in space around the Milky Way, dinosaurs ruled the Earth. In fact, this sun orbit has only happened 20.4 times since the sun itself formed 4.6 billion years ago.

Since the sun is 26,000 light-years from the centre of the Milky Way, it has to travel at an astonishing speed of 782,000 km/h in a circular orbit around the Milky Way centre. Just for comparison, the Earth is rotating at a speed of 1,770 km/h and it is moving at a speed of 108,000 km/h around the sun.

It's estimated that the sun will continue fusing hydrogen for another 7 billon years or so. In other words, it only has another 31 orbits it can make before it runs out of fuel.

Astonishing fact

If a drop sized matter from the core of the sun is placed on the surface of the Earth, no living organism will survive for a distance of 150 km from that drop.

Astonishing fact

The surface area of sun is equivalent to that of 11,990 Earths!

Solar space missions

Astronomers study the sun using special instruments. Scientists analyze how and why the amount of light from the sun varies over time, the effect of the sun's light on the Earth's climate, spectral lines, the sun's magnetic field, the solar wind, and many other solar phenomena. The outer regions of the sun (the corona) are studied during solar eclipses.

The first satellites designed to observe the sun were NASA's Pioneers 5, 6, 7, 8 and 9, which were launched between 1959 and 1968. These probes orbited the sun at a distance similar to that of the Earth, and made the first detailed measurements of the solar wind and the solar magnetic field. Pioneer 9 operated for a particularly long time, transmitting data until May 1983.

In the 1970s, two Helios spacecraft and the Skylab Apollo Telescope Mount provided scientists with significant new data on solar wind and the solar corona. The Helios 1 and 2 probes studied the solar wind from an orbit carrying the spacecraft inside Mercury's orbit at perihelion.

In 1980, the Solar Maximum Mission was launched by NASA. This spacecraft was designed to observe gamma rays, X-rays and UV radiation from solar flares during a time of high solar activity and solar luminosity. The Solar Maximum Mission subsequently acquired thousands of images of the solar corona before re-entering the Earth's atmosphere in June 1989.

Launched in 1991, Japan's Yohkoh (sunbeam) satellite observed solar flares at X-ray wavelengths. Yohkoh observed an entire solar cycle but went into standby mode when an annular eclipse in 2001 caused it to lose its lock on the sun. It was destroyed by atmospheric re-entry in 2005.

One of the most important solar missions till date has been the Solar and Heliospheric Observatory (SOHO), jointly built by the European Space Agency and NASA and launched on 2 December, 1995. It has proven to be so useful that a follow-on mission, the Solar Dynamics Observatory was launched in February, 2010. Situated at the **Lagrangian point** between the Earth and the sun (at which the gravitational pull from both is equal), SOHO has provided a constant view of the sun at many wavelengths since its launch. Besides its direct solar observation, SOHO has enabled the discovery of a large number of comets, mostly very tiny sun grazing comets which incinerate as they pass the sun.

Astonishing fact

The volume of sun is equivalent to the volume of 1.3 million Earths.

All these satellites have observed the sun from the plane of the ecliptic, and so have only observed its equatorial regions in detail. The Ulysses probe was launched in 1990 to study the sun's Polar Regions. Once Ulysses was in its scheduled orbit, it began observing the solar wind and magnetic field strength at high solar latitudes, finding that the solar wind from high latitudes was moving at about 750 km/s which were slower than expected, and that there were large magnetic waves emerging from high latitudes which scattered galactic cosmic rays.

Elemental abundances in the photosphere are well-known from spectroscopic studies, but the composition of the interior of the sun is more poorly understood. A solar wind sample return mission, Genesis, was designed to allow astronomers to directly measure the composition of solar material. Genesis returned to Earth in 2004 but was damaged by a crash landing after its parachute failed to deploy on re-entry into Earth's atmosphere. Despite severe damage, some usable samples have been recovered from the spacecraft's sample return module and are undergoing analysis.

The Solar Terrestrial Relations Observatory (STEREO) mission was launched in October 2006. Two identical spacecrafts were launched into orbits that caused them to (respectively) pull further ahead of and fall gradually behind the Earth. This enabled stereoscopic imaging of the sun and solar phenomena, such as coronal mass ejections.

Astonishing fact

A man weighing 60 kg in the Earth will weigh 1680 kg in the sun.

Sun in culture

The sun is the star at the centre of the solar system and all the planets orbit around it. Most life on Earth evolved with the sun in mind; the rising and setting sun defined the cycle of daily life. Ancient peoples were entirely dependent on the sun for light; only the light from a full moon gave any way to see in the night. It wasn't until the invention of fire that humans had any way to get any work done after the sun went down.

Since the sun was such an important object, many ancient people treated it with reverence and considered the sun a god. Many worshipped the sun, and built monuments to celebrate it. Monuments like Stonehenge in England, and the Pyramids of Egypt were used to mark the position of the sun over the course of the year.

It was long thought that the sun orbited around the Earth, but it was Nicolaus Copernicus who first proposed a sun-centered Solar System. This theory gained evidence from Galileo and other early astronomers. By the 1800s, solar astronomy was very advanced, with astronomers carefully tracking sunspots, measuring absorption lines in the spectrum of light from the sun, and discovering infrared.

Proxima Centauri is the closest star around the sun, at a distance of 4.3 light years.

Astonishing fact

The sun is orbited by nine major planets– Mercury, Venus, Earth, Mars, Jupiter, Saturn, Uranus, Neptune, and Pluto (no longer an official planet).

Humans have long recognized the sun's role in supporting life on Earth, and as a result many societies throughout history have paid homage to the sun by giving it prominent roles in their religions and mythologies.

The sun is sometimes referred to by its Latin name **Sol** or by its Greek name **Helios**. Its astrological and astronomical symbol is a circle with a point at its centre. The ancient Greeks grouped the sun together with the other celestial bodies which moved across the sky, calling them all planets.

The religious significance of the sun has its roots in the very earliest of recorded Western history. Both the ancient Greeks and ancient Romans worshipped one or more solar deities.

Many Greek myths personify the sun as a Titan named Helios, who wore a shining crown and rode a chariot across the sky, causing day. The Roman Empire adopted Helios into their own mythology and changed its name to Sol. The title Sol Invictus ('the undefeated sun') was applied to several solar deities and depicted on several types of Roman coins during the 3rd and 4th centuries.

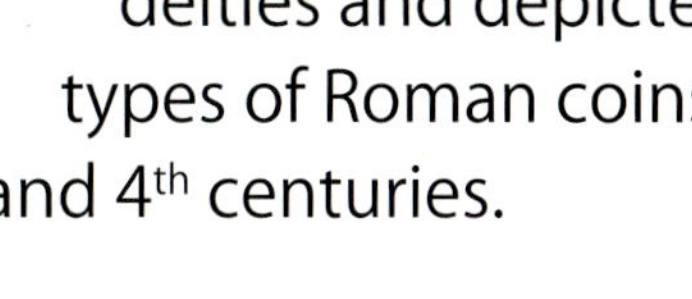

Sun god Ra

The sun was also worshipped in many pre-Columbian societies in the Americas, including the Incas and the Aztecs.

The worship of the sun in the Eastern world has its historical origin in Ancient Egypt. The Egyptians identified the sun with **Ra**, one of the major deities in their religion.

In Hindu religious literature, the sun is notably mentioned as the visible form of God that one can see every day. In Hinduism, **Surya** is the chief solar deity. Many scripts from Hindu mythology referred the sun as a King, who rides on a chariot of seven horses (this is indication of seven colours from sunlight).

In the Quran, the Islamic religious scripture, the sun like other celestial objects is not endowed with any particular religious significance or symbolic meaning. Due to the widespread presence of sun-worshiping cults in Pre-Islamic Arabia, Muslim doctrine, the Shariah forbade all prayers during the rising and setting of the sun, to symbolically refute its divinity.

Pre-Islamic Arab pagans considered solar eclipses and other celestial occurrences as omens signalling the passing of an important figure or other Earthly events. However, this belief was refuted explicitly by Prophet Muhammad in the year 632 C.E, when the death of his son coincided with a solar eclipse: 'The sun and the Moon are from among the evidences of God. They do not eclipse because of someone's death or life.'

Unlike the Earth, the sun is completely gaseous; there is no solid surface on the sun.

Surya

The fate of the sun

The sun has been shining for about 4.5 billion years. The size of the sun is a balance between the outward pressure made by the release of energy from nuclear fusion and the inward pull of gravity. Over its 4.5 billion years of life, the sun's radius has increased about 6 per cent bigger. It has enough hydrogen fuel to burn for about 10 billion years, meaning it has a bit over 5 billion years left, and during this time it will continue to expand at the same rate.

When the core runs out of hydrogen fuel, it will contract under the weight of gravity. However, some hydrogen fusion will occur in the upper layers. As the core contracts, it heats up and this heats the upper layers causing them to expand. As the outer layers expand, the radius of the sun will increase and it will become a **red giant**, an elderly star.

The radius of the red giant sun will be 100 times of what it is now, lying just beyond the Earth's orbit, so the Earth will plunge into the core of the red giant sun and be vapourised. At some point after this, the core will become hot enough to cause the helium to fuse into carbon.

When the helium fuel will be exhausted, the core will expand and cool. The upper layers will expand and eject material. Finally, the core will cool into a **white dwarf**.

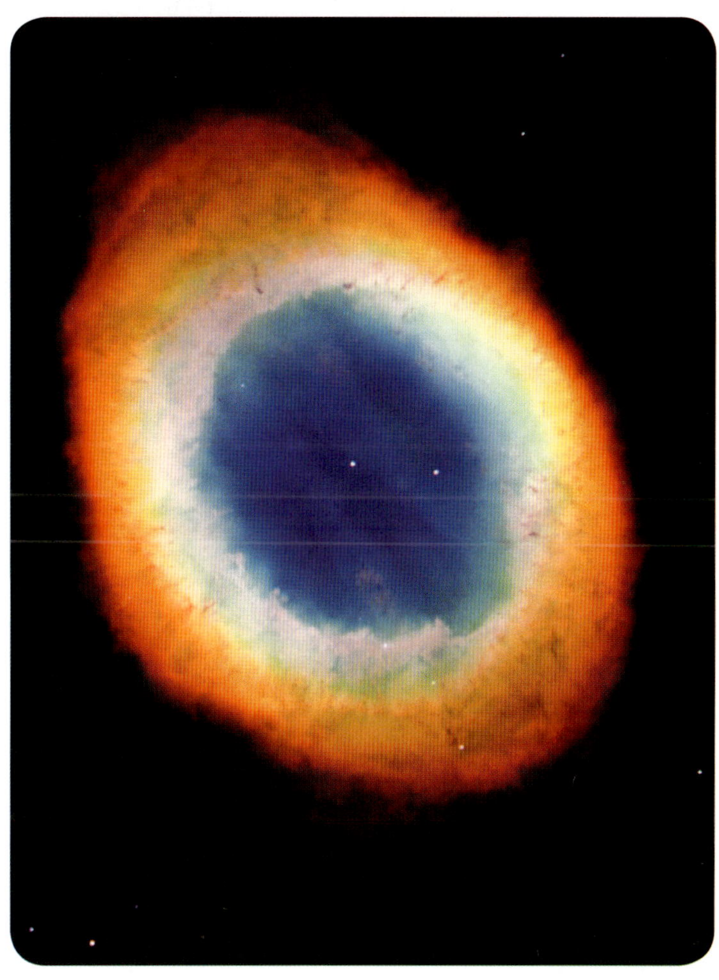

Eventually, it will further cool into a nearly invisible **black dwarf**. This entire process will take a few billion years.

Astonishing fact

100,000,000,000 tons of dynamite would have to be detonated every second to match the energy produced by the sun.

Astonishing fact

In ancient Egypt, the sun God Ra was the dominant figure among the high gods. He achieved the highest status because he was believed to have created himself and eight other gods.

What the sun does for us

The sun keeps us in place. Even though the Earth is located approximately 140 million km away from the sun, the sun's gravity can reach out and hang onto us. Without this pull of gravity, we would just fly off into space, away from the warmth and light of the sun, and out into the cold black of space. This is a very important job that the sun does for us, and makes everything else possible.

The sun helps with the tides. Most of the daily ocean tides happen because of the moon. But we experience our highest and lowest tides when the sun, Earth and moon are lined up in a row.

The sun causes the weather. The sun is constantly heating up the planet. But it's not always heating the same parts of the planet at the same time. It's these differences that create the weather. When one part of the Earth is warm like the land, and another part is cold like the oceans, air moves from one region to the other creating winds. When the sun heats water, it evaporates, becoming clouds and eventually falls again as rain. We wouldn't have weather without the sun.

The sun gives us energy. In addition to the heat we receive from the sun, plants absorb energy from the sun, mix this with carbon dioxide in the atmosphere, and grow. All of the fossil fuels we use to run our modern economy come from energy from the sun, stored over millions of years.

Test Your MEMORY

1. What is the sun?
2. Write briefly about the formation of the sun.
3. Write about the layers of the sun.
4. Write about the sun's magnetic field.
5. Write two characteristics of the sun.
6. What are sunspots?
7. What is a solar eclipse?
8. What is sunlight?
9. Write briefly about the sun's orbit?
10. Write about the solar space missions.
11. How is the sun portrayed in various culture?
12. What is the fate of the sun?

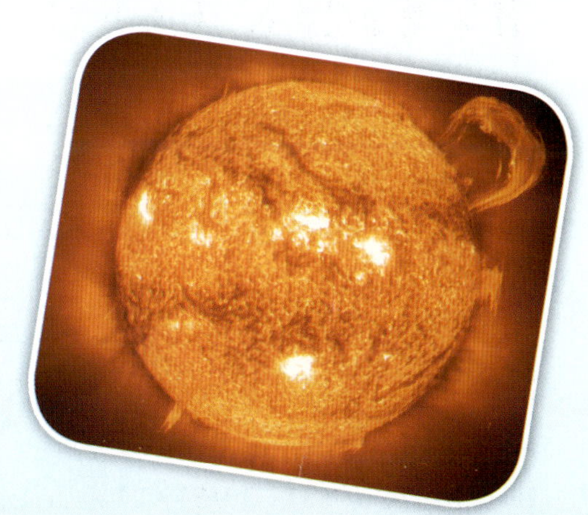

Index

A

asteroids 3
astronomers 5, 6, 21, 22, 23, 25, 26
Astronomical Unit (AU) 7, 11, 20

C

carbon 10, 29, 30
chromosphere 7, 8, 14
comets 3, 15, 24
convective zone 7
core 7, 12, 22, 29
corona 7, 8, 14, 16, 18, 23
coronal mass ejections 4, 8, 16, 25

E

electromagnetic radiation 13, 19
electromagnetic waves 12
electrons 13, 15

G

gamma rays 12, 23

H

helium 3, 5, 10, 15, 29
hydrogen 3, 5, 6, 10, 15, 22, 29

I

infrared rays 13
iron 10
interplanetary magnetic field 9

L

light year 11

M

magnesium 10
meteoroids 3
milky way 4, 11, 22

N

neon 10
nitrogen 10

O

oxygen 10, 20

P

particle radiation 13
penumbra 17, 18
photosphere 7, 8, 17, 25
photosynthesis 3, 20
plasma 10
protons 13

R

radiation 7, 8, 12, 13, 19, 23
radiative zone 7

S

silicon 10
sol 27
solar eclipse 18, 28, 31
solar energy 20
solar flare 14
solar flares 4, 8, 9, 14, 16, 23, 24
solar prominence 16
solar wind 15
spectrum of light 13, 26
sunspots 8, 17
solar constant 20

U

umbra 17, 18

About the series:

What are the things that exist in space? What is the Sun, Moon and the Earth made up of? What is a star? All such questions that kids ask have been answered here.

Titles in this series:

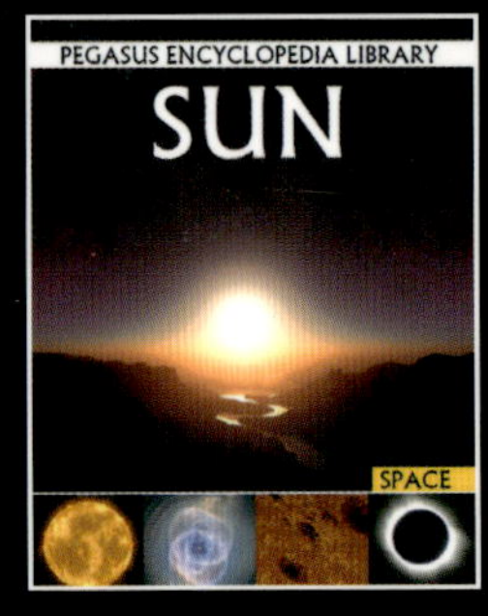

Pegasus
An imprint of
B. Jain Publishers (P) Ltd.
USA – EUROPE – INDIA
Web: www.bjain.com

US$ 5.95
ISBN: 978-81-319-1289-8
9 788131 912898
009000

Spanking Tails 3
"Much too Cheeky!"
Edward
A Gallery Girls Collection

SPANKING TAILS 3 - FEATURING THE CHEEK-WARMING ARTWORK OF:

Luis Buci

Mitch Byrd

Diego Cirulli

Federico Combi

Javier Cosacarelli

J.L. Czerniawski

Alejandro Ferrero

Gonzalo Flores

Diego Florio

Danilo Guida

Pablo Kousovitis

Brian LeBlanc

Juan Lencina

Anibal Maraschi

Percy Ochoa

Federico Ossio

Perla Pilucki

Emiliano Urdinola

Front Cover Painting by **Edward Ree**

Back Cover Painting by **Brian LeBlan**